Victorian Homes

Brenda Williams

Heinemann

www.heinemann.co.uk/library
Visit our website to find out more information about **Heinemann Library** books.

To order:
☎ Phone 44 (0) 1865 888066
▤ Send a fax to 44 (0) 1865 314091
💻 Visit the Heinemann Bookshop at www.heinemann.co.uk/library to browse our catalogue and order online.

First published in Great Britain by Heinemann Library, Halley Court, Jordan Hill, Oxford OX2 8EJ, part of Harcourt Education.

Heinemann is a registered trademark of Harcourt Education Ltd.

© Harcourt Education Ltd 2003
First published in paperback in 2004
The moral right of the proprietor has been asserted.

Editorial: Lucy Thunder and Helen Cox
Design: Jo Hinton-Malivoire, Richard Parker and Tinstar Design Limited (www.tinstar.co.uk)
Picture Research: Rebecca Sodergren
Production: Séverine Ribierre

Originated by Ambassador Litho Ltd
Printed in China by WKT Company Ltd

ISBN 0 431 14623 3 (hardback)
07 06 05 04 03
10 9 8 7 6 5 4 3 2 1

ISBN 0 431 14633 0 (paperback)
08 07 06 05 04
10 9 8 7 6 5 4 3 2 1

British Library Cataloguing in Publication Data
Williams, Brenda
Victorian Homes. – (People in the past)
640.9'41'09034
A full catalogue record for this book is available from the British Library.

Acknowledgements
The publishers would like to thank the following for permission to reproduce photographs: Billie Love Historical Collection **pp.18**, **20**, **31**; Bridgeman Art Archive **pp. 17**, **28**, **29**; Collections/Oliver Benn **p. 5**, /Paul Felix **p. 13**; English Heritage **pp. 9**, **42**; Geffrye Musuem **p. 22**; Kelmscott Museum/Society of Antiquarians of London **p. 23**; Mary Evans Picture Library **pp. 10**, **11**, **16**, **25**, **33**, **34**, **36**, **37**, **39**, **41**; Museum of English Rural Life **p. 8**; Saltaire Village Society **p. 15**; Victoria and Albert Museum **pp. 6**, **26**, **27**.

The publishers would like to thank Rebecca Vickers for her assistance with the preparation of this book.

Every effort has been made to contact copyright holders of any material reproduced in this book. Any omissions will be rectified in subsequent printings if notice is given to the publishers.

MA	MB	MC
MD	ME	MF
MG	MH	MM
MN	MO	MR
AB	MT	MW

Contents

Words appearing in the text in bold, **like this**, are explained in the Glossary.

The Victorian age

The Victorian age is named after Queen Victoria. She became Britain's queen in 1837 and reigned until her death in 1901. During her long reign, Britain became the richest and most powerful nation in the world. The **British Empire** included a quarter of the world's land and people. Many British homes contained reminders of this vast empire – such as maps, pictures, empire-made goods or souvenirs of travel abroad. Yet for most people 'home, sweet home' was what really mattered.

Victorian times

During Queen Victoria's life, Britain went through startling changes. Its population more than doubled in 100 years, from 15 million in 1801 to over 37 million by 1901. The Victorians lived through an **Industrial Revolution**, during which many people moved from the country to the towns, to work in factories. In 1801, only about 30 per cent of British people lived in towns, but this figure had shot up to around 80 per cent by 1901. For most Victorian families, home meant a house in the town, not a country cottage.

Victorians were proud of the British Empire, which was ruled by Queen Victoria. This map from the time shows the countries of the empire in red.

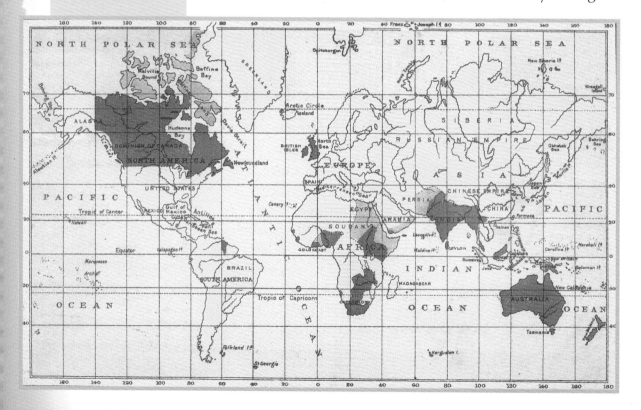

Victorian houses today in Ealing, London. The rooms inside may have been updated, but the outsides of the houses still look much as they did in the 1800s when they were built.

Victorians at home

Generally, the richer you were the bigger your home was. Very poor people often lived in tiny cottages or **slums**. Richer people could also afford to pay servants to help with the housework, or buy new labour-saving **gadgets.** Servants had their own rooms in wealthy households, usually at the top of the house.

Houses in 1900 were very different from homes in 1800. By 1900, some homes had amazing new inventions, such as electric light, telephones and **gramophones.** There were no automatic washing machines, microwaves, freezers or televisions in homes, however.

Victorian money

In Victorian times people counted up their money in pounds (£), shillings (s) and pennies (d). There were 20 shillings in 1 pound, and 12 pennies in 1 shilling. A woman spent 3d (just over 1p) a week on potatoes to feed a family of five.

Victoriana today

Some people today call Victorian things 'Victoriana'. They enjoy taking a fresh look at Victorian homes, or even copying Victorian designs. This book will show you round the homes of rich and poor families. Our **evidence** comes not only from what people wrote and the pictures they made, but also from the buildings themselves. People still live in houses put up by Victorian builders, so let's start our exploration of what life was like for Victorian families at home.

The family home

Home was the centre of Victorian family life. People ate together, spent the evening together and (since many families were large) children often slept together. The Victorians liked to think of home as a place of comfort, safety and above all privacy. Yet rich people, with servants in the house, had less privacy than we do. Poor families had hardly any. Their homes were cramped, and at night some slept four or more in a bed and shared a toilet with their neighbours.

A morning room in a **middle-class** home, photographed in 1865. This was a woman's room. Here she wrote letters or sewed, read a book, gave the maidservant her instructions and entertained women friends.

Paying the rent

Most people in Victorian times did not own their homes. Instead, they paid **rent** to the owner of the rooms, cottage or house in which they lived. The owner, called a landlord, might own just one or two houses, or a good many. Out of a **farm labourer's** weekly wage of 10 shillings (50p), the rent for a cottage in the 1880s varied from 1 to 2 shillings (5 to 10p). The landlord might be a shopkeeper, a farmer, a factory owner or a builder. A builder would buy a plot of land and build two or three houses on it. He might then sell the homes to a landlord or rent them out himself.

Public and private rooms

There were three parts to a wealthy Victorian home: the public, the private and the 'not to be mentioned'. The public rooms were the hall, drawing room, dining room and morning room. Here guests and visitors would be greeted and entertained. The family's private rooms were the bedrooms, the master's study and, in a big house, the dressing rooms where he and his wife got dressed. Just as private in a way were the kitchen and the servants' rooms, because the owners did not often venture into them. 'Not to be mentioned' were the bathroom and toilet (if there was one indoors).

Keeping up to date

In 1851, visitors to the **Great Exhibition** in London were eager to see an ideal home. Books and magazines informed them what was modern yet tasteful. Advertisements showed what a little money could buy – a piano perhaps, or an elegant table. Writing in 1851, a doctor wondered what people in the future would make of 'a modern drawing room, with its sumptuous furniture of velvet, silk, glass, gold, china and rosewood … ' He thought 'they would hardly understand its **paraphernalia** and appointments'. In a way he was right. We have to understand the Victorians to see why their homes looked the way they did.

Rich and poor homes

In Victorian Britain, neither the government nor **local councils** built houses. People had to find their own homes. A poor **farm labourer's** home might be a cottage, with two or three small rooms. For a clerk in the city, home might be a rented **terraced house** or one room in a **tenement** building.

Anywhere but the workhouse

For the jobless and penniless, the only home was often the **workhouse.** Here the poor were given a bed and food in return for work. Some workhouses were well run. A French visitor to a Manchester workhouse in 1862 wrote that, 'there is no smell; the beds are almost white … this was a palace compared with the kennels in which the poor dwell'. Nevertheless, he added 'The workhouse is regarded as a prison; the poor consider it a point of honour not to go there.'

Poor people's homes

Poor people had little money to spend on home comforts and many lived in homes that were practically falling down. Many country people lived in small cottages, some built in Tudor times or earlier.

A Victorian labourer's cottage was simply furnished, with wooden tables, stools and cupboards. A bedroom usually had space for two single beds, a storage chest and chair.

Visitors to Osborne House today can see the rooms that Queen Victoria's family lived in. The rooms were cheerful and bright. As a modern touch, the builders put in brick floors and cement **skirtings** to reduce the risk of fire.

As late as 1893, a government official reported that around Maldon in Essex cottages were 'fearfully cold in winter' and so draughty that 'often in winter the candle or lamp is blown out'. Some bedroom floors had holes covered over with bits of wood and a doctor once visited an old man who had slipped into a hole and broken his leg!

The homes of the better-off

A **middle-class** shopkeeper might live in one of the new **suburbs**, in a trim brick house, with small front and back gardens. The very rich lived in large town houses or old country mansions. Factory owners built themselves new mansions, with modern conveniences and iron railings to keep out unwanted visitors.

The Queen's favourite home

In 1845, Queen Victoria and Prince Albert bought Osborne House on the Isle of Wight. The Queen was delighted: 'The rooms are small but very nice. With some few alterations and additions for the children it might be made an excellent house'. Prince Albert asked a London builder, Thomas Cubitt, to modernize, redecorate and add on new rooms, and the royal family moved there in September 1846. It became Queen Victoria's favourite house.

Living in the city

The **factory** age begun by the **Industrial Revolution** changed home life in Britain for ever. Victorian towns and cities grew very quickly, often in an unplanned way. Small towns like Birmingham became big cities in Victorian times.

Homes grow in fields

From the 1840s, new railways were built into city centres. Often this meant that builders knocked down old **medieval** streets to make room. Most cities still had patches of green, and even farms, in the middle of town.

London grew bigger and faster than any other city, as the new railways sucked in surrounding country towns like Bromley and Croydon. Looking at South London in the mid-1800s, Charles Masterman (later a Member of Parliament) saw only 'populated streets, roads labelled, a little packed maze of little packed houses … tiny backyards in which a woman can just turn round'. Fields and farms had been swallowed up by rows of **terraced houses**.

This picture by the French artist Gustave Doré shows a gloomy view of Victorian London. Houses with tiny backyards are crammed together. Smoke from chimneys and steam railways fills the air. In a terrace, each house held up its neighbours – though in badly built rows, the house on the end sometimes fell down!

Many small towns became suburbs of fast-growing cities. People who could afford it escaped from the smoke and smells of the inner city by moving to newly built houses in the leafy suburbs.

Slums and suburbs

As more people crowded into the cities, many ended up living in **slums**. In Liverpool, thousands of people lived in cellars. At night, rats scuttled out from the rotten floorboards, through which rose a stink of sewage from the **cesspit** beneath. In London, dozens of families often lived crammed into one building, known as a 'rookery'. Rooks are birds, and hundreds crowd together to nest in a few trees known as a rookery. People too poor even for a rookery slept in a lodging house, where for a penny or two they shared a flea-ridden bed with someone else. In these conditions disease spread quickly.

People who could pay a higher **rent** were glad to move out to the **suburbs.** Some travelled by train or horse bus to work in the town, but many people walked. Only rich town-dwellers kept a horse and carriage.

Inside a rookery

In 1848, investigators went into the rookeries close to London's Oxford Street. They found that a typical two-room 'nest' housed five families; a total of nineteen people. The investigators found the 'state of rooms and furniture was bad, dirty; state of windows, six whole panes and ten broken. Number of beds six. This room opens into the yard, 6 feet (2m) square, which is covered over with night soil [waste from the toilet].'

Country cottages

On visiting Leicestershire in 1830, the writer William Cobbett found 'hovels, made of mud and straw'. Inside were 'wretched boards tacked together to serve as a table'. Not all country homes were so wretched. In Surrey and Sussex, he saw well-made oak chests, beds and tables in country cottages. These were signs 'of plain manners and plentiful living'. Cobbett was old-fashioned. He disapproved of padded sofas and carpets, which were becoming fashionable.

Peering into the cottage gloom

Around the British Isles, cottages were built in different styles from local materials such as stone, flint, chalk, brick or cob (a mixture of mud and straw). Few were as neat and clean as the homes we see in Victorian paintings. In 1849, Alexander Mackay wrote a newspaper article about a two-roomed country cottage in Buckinghamshire.

'The cabin is so rude and uncouth that it has less the appearance of being built than of having been suddenly thrown up out of the ground.' The walls were of sandstone 'fast crumbling to decay' and 'the **thatch** is thickly encrusted with a bright green vegetation'. Inside, it was so dark he could barely see. There was only one window. This cottage was home to a family of nine, who slept in the one room upstairs.

Tied cottages

For some workers, home was a 'tied cottage'. Tied cottages were owned by the worker's employer, and let out to the worker for a low **rent**. Most workers would rather pay the full rent for their own cottage, if they could. A worker forced to live in a tied cottage was 'tied' to the job. If he lost his job, he also lost his home: 'out they goes, neck and crop, bag and baggage', as people said at the time.

Most country people loved flowers and grew them in their cottage gardens.

Cold and dark

Many cottages around Britain were just as small, dark, cold and overcrowded. Stone or dirt floors were often so uneven that a three-legged stool was a more stable seat than a chair. To give some privacy, bedrooms were divided by curtains, but big boys often slept downstairs. Some were 'boarded out' to a family whose children had left home. Some rich landowners built 'model villages' for their **farm labourers**, with clean and airy new cottages. However, there were never enough of these new homes.

The family pig

At the back of many cottages was a pigsty where the family kept a pig. The pig was fed on anything from kitchen leftovers to snails picked out of the hedgerow. When it had been fattened and killed, the pig provided a family with pork, bacon, black pudding, sausages and pies. There would be a 'pig feast' at which meat was shared with neighbours who had helped care for the animal.

Industrial housing

Many industrial towns grew rapidly in the first half of the 19th century. **Factory** owners wanted their workers to live within earshot of the hooter that was sounded at the start of the working day. So they built workers' houses close to the factory.

Building slum houses

The new industrial homes were cheap but poorly built, 'back to back'. This meant that two houses were more or less stuck together, with no gardens and not much light or fresh air either. Like a cottage, the worker's home had a living room and **scullery** downstairs, with two small bedrooms upstairs. At the back was an outhouse, which served as a **privy** and coal-store.

Workers' homes were built of brick, with a roof of slates or tiles. Many builders used cheap materials, and their poorly built houses either fell down, or soon became rotten and leaky **slums**. Few had toilets, drains or tap water. Water drawn from the pump for drinking was dirty and carried germs. There were no **sewers**. In the 1840s–1850s, outbreaks of **cholera**, carried by diseased water, killed thousands of people in the cities. In 1868 and 1875, laws were passed to provide clean water and knock down unhealthy slum homes.

This picture shows the slum area of Church Lane, London, in the 1870s. Gradually, the worst of these slum houses were cleared away, and replaced by more modern homes.

Making homes healthier

A London doctor called John Snow showed that cholera was caused by drinking water polluted by waste from toilets. In 1854, he traced an outbreak of the disease to a public well, the Broad Street Pump in Soho. When he took the handle off the pump, people could not use it and fewer became ill. His findings shocked the government into building new water pipes and sewers.

Model homes

Some well-meaning factory owners set about building better homes for their employees. Robert Owen (1771–1858) built a 'model' (ideal) cotton mill, with homes and a school, at New Lanark in Scotland. Examples of model homes for workers were shown at the **Great Exhibition** of 1851.

Titus Salt, a Bradford wool-mill owner, built decent homes for his workers between 1853 and 1876. The chocolate-makers George and Richard Cadbury did the same on their Bournville estate in Birmingham, begun in 1879. New building laws meant that by 1900, most industrial homes were at least sturdy, dry and had clean running water.

This is Peabody Square in Westminster, London, in 1869. 'Peabody buildings' were paid for by an American banker called George Peabody. He believed working people deserved decent homes.

At home in the suburbs

A life in the **suburbs** was the dream of many Victorian families. There they could live in a house with a front and back garden. 'An Englishman's home is his castle' was a popular saying, and inside his home, the Victorian man felt he was king.

Behind the front door

Behind the front door of a typical **middle-class** home, with its shiny brass doorknocker, was the hall and its doormat (no muddy feet allowed). Here, on the hallstand, people left their coats, hats, umbrellas and walking sticks. A door led downstairs to the cellar. Other doors led to the kitchen, at the back, and into the front **parlour**, the drawing room and the dining room. Larger homes might also have a smoking room, for men, and a **conservatory**, with potted plants. The man of the house could retire to his study with its bookshelves, desk and armchair. The mantelpiece over the fireplace was a good place to keep pipes, matches and the chiming clock that told him when it was nearly dinner time.

A middle-class family was waited on at meal times by the house maid. Many better-off families also had paid cooks.

This picture shows a Victorian family in their drawing room – short for 'withdrawing' room. In the evenings, ladies withdrew from the dining room to the drawing room after dinner, leaving the men to their drinks, cigars and 'men's talk'.

Upstairs and downstairs

Upstairs were the bedrooms and, at the top of the house, a small room for a servant. A Victorian family with enough money to **rent** a home in the suburbs could usually afford at least one servant. Her day began at 6 a.m., as she heated water for washing and shaving, and carried the jugs upstairs to the family's bedrooms.

The maid also opened the front door to callers. Often the hall was the only part of the house that a casual caller would see. Its floor might be covered with the new invention, **linoleum**. The walls were sometimes half-tiled and perhaps decorated – with a hunting scene, maybe, or a stuffed trout in a glass case.

Come into the parlour

The parlour was the 'best room' in the house, with the most expensive furniture and finest fireplace. It was often filled with 'knick-knacks', the sort of souvenirs and cheap ornaments that a writer in *The Lady* magazine of 1884 called disapprovingly 'trumpery bric-a-brac'. Family photos were ranged on shelves, alongside china animals, jugs, dried flowers, seashells and holiday souvenirs. The parlour was always kept ready for visitors.

Stately homes

The very rich lived in great houses. Some were very old, while others were newly built. **Medieval** castles were popular places to live, though they were usually damp and draughty. Some wealthy Victorians built themselves grand 'modern' castles, equipped with gaslights and bathrooms. A few of the most splendid Victorian houses are open to visitors today.

Living in style

Baron Ferdinand de Rothschild was a rich banker who built Waddesdon Manor in Buckinghamshire in the 1870s. A railway track was built to carry in stone for the grand house, which looked like a French chateau (castle), with French furniture inside. Outside, half-grown trees were dragged into the new park by teams of horses. The Baron even had his own orchestra and a private zoo.

This photograph is of Charlton House, the large home of Lord Hobhouse. It shows the family in their garden taking the air.

Another remarkable house was Cragside in Northumberland. It was built between 1870 and 1885 for Lord Armstrong, a factory owner. He not only had a fireplace big enough to sit in, and a magnificent view, but also electricity from a water-powered generator. Cragside was one of the first homes in Britain with electric light. Lord Armstrong was a friend of Joseph Swan, inventor of Britain's first light bulb.

Running the house

Visitors wandering around such enormous mansions today might wonder how these big houses were run. It took a lot of hard work, mostly carried out by a small army of servants. The biggest houses employed as many as 50 servants. Most were busy in the house, others worked in the gardens and on the estate. Servants came when called by the ringing of bell-pulls, which were in most rooms. They had to hurry along corridors and climb lots of stairs since few houses had lifts (as Cragside did). Some had pulley-worked **hoists** to carry food up from the kitchen. The kitchen was often so far away from the dining room that hot food must have gone cold by the time it reached the table.

House parties

The owner and his wife often had separate bedrooms and **dressing rooms**. To house weekend parties of 30 or more guests during the hunting or shooting seasons, rich house-owners added more bedrooms. They turned parlours into **billiard rooms** or **gunrooms**. Some even had new bathrooms fitted, using steam engines to pump hot water around the house.

Opening the stable door

Many rich families kept a carriage and horses. There were various kinds of carriage, from a two-wheeled gig to a four-wheeled barouche. Big houses had buildings called stables to house these vehicles and the horses that pulled them. By 1900, carriages were being replaced by shiny, but smelly, new cars.

Building a home

Some people, especially in the countryside, built their own homes. Most homes, however, were built by local builders, who hired skilled workers such as bricklayers and carpenters.

Work in progress

Work began by digging a hole, which became a cellar for coal or storage. Then the builder would lay foundations of brick, or rubbish such as broken pottery. Brick was so commonly used for house building that machines were invented to make bricks faster. The colour of bricks varied around the country and local bricks gave homes local colour. London walls were yellowish, while those in Staffordshire were blue-grey.

The higher the house, the thinner were its walls. This saved weight and bricks. Most houses were only two or three storeys high. **Terraced houses** needed fewer bricks, because they shared side walls, and is one reason why they were popular with Victorian builders.

This photo shows Victorian builders at work. Most of the materials they used were produced locally.

Do it yourself

A funny book called *The Diary of a Nobody*, published in 1892 by George and Weedon Grossmith, gives this account of Victorian DIY by its hero, Mr Pooter. 'There is always something to be done; a tin tack here, a Venetian blind to put straight, a fan to nail up, a carpet to nail down – all of which I can do with my pipe in my mouth.' For larger jobs, such as painting or wallpapering, the Victorians called in a local tradesman.

Fixtures and fittings

Floors were made of timber boards, though stone or tiled floors were often laid in downstairs rooms and hallways. Ceilings and walls were plastered and then whitewashed with a white-lime mixture. Plaster mouldings to decorate ceilings were made in local workshops. So were the windows, wooden front door and staircase. These were usually more decorative than today's styles.

Many houses had gas pipes for gas lighting. Although the first electric cables were being installed by the 1880s, gas was still popular until the early 1900s.

Roofs and windows

Most houses had roofs of slates, cut from a slate quarry, or of factory-made clay tiles. The roof was pitched (sloped) to let rain drain off into iron gutters. Some country homes had **thatched** roofs. A thatch of straw lasted about 25 years. Reed thatch cost more, but could last for a hundred years.

Sash windows, which slide up and down on cords, were popular. Bay windows, extending out from the walls, made house fronts look bigger and let in more light. To make a house look fashionably 'medieval', builders added turrets and pointed-arch windows.

Victorian furniture

The poorest country homes had little furniture other than a simple wooden table, chairs or stools. Instead of a rug or carpet, poor people put down a **rush mat** or an old potato sack on the floor. Family treasures, such as a rocking chair or **pewter** plates, were handed on from parents to children.

Better-off Victorians liked a variety of furniture styles: French, **medieval**, Tudor, the 'home-made' Arts and Crafts look, even Chinese and Japanese. Most furniture was made of solid wood, though plywood, which was lighter and cheaper, became more common from the 1850s.

Solid to sit and sleep on

Almost all Victorian furniture was dark and shiny – the result of daily polishing. Bedroom furniture, often made from oak and mahogany wood, was solid and heavy. Light bamboo and cane were used for small tables and hall hat-stands.

The Victorians liked enormous wardrobes in their bedrooms, with massive **sideboards** and dressers in their dining rooms and kitchens.

Some wealthy Victorians slept on feather mattresses in four-poster beds with side-curtains drawn at night to keep out draughts.

Victorian furniture was often made in a factory, copying more expensive foreign styles. This little 'occasional' table would have decorated a typical Victorian sitting room, along with gas lamps, a fireplace, dark wallpaper and heavy wooden furniture.

By 1900, brass or iron bedsteads with wire bases and sprung mattresses were far more common. Home-made **patchwork quilts** and eiderdowns (duvets) kept people warm on winter nights.

Expensive padded chairs and sofas, at first stuffed with horsehair, but later with metal springs, were kept for the best rooms. To stop men's macassar tree-oil hair lotion from staining chairs, linen squares known as 'anti-macassars' were placed on chair backs. Fringed or frilly cloths were hung over tables and pianos, and from the mantelpiece above the fire.

Handmade or factory made?

Poor families often bought a wooden chair or table from a local carpenter, or even made their own. Factories made furniture sold in shops. Travelling workers known as 'bodgers' cut timber in beech woods, and shaped chair legs and stretchers (crosspieces). They took the pieces to the factory, where other workers made chair seats and backs. Lastly, 'framers' put the chairs together.

In 1845, Thomas Jordan invented a woodcarving machine, to speed up furniture making. This made it cheaper and people began buying lots more factory-made furniture.

The Morris chair, made by William Morris' company but designed by Philip Webb.

The Arts and Crafts Movement

An artist named William Morris (1834–96) hated factory-made furniture as much as he loved to buy medieval art. He wanted to make furniture in older styles, by using older methods. So, in 1861, he started a company to hand-make furniture, wallpaper, tapestries and stained glass. His 'Arts and Crafts' products were admired, but were too expensive for ordinary working people to buy.

Decoration and ornaments

To our eyes, a Victorian room would look very cluttered. William Morris wrote in 1879: 'I have never been into a rich man's house which would not have looked the better having a bonfire made outside it of nine-tenths of all that it held.'

People filled every space and shelf in a room. There were clocks, china jugs and vases, pottery animals, brass candlesticks, pet birds in cages, and dead butterflies in glass cases. There were plants in pots and flowers in window boxes. Many rooms had ceiling decorations made of plaster, or flowery designs in papier-mâché which was so light that no one got hurt if a decoration came unstuck and fell down!

Clocks and china

Almost every family had a clock. Timepieces came in all shapes and sizes: there were tall long case or grandfather clocks, 'skeleton clocks' inside a clear glass case, and cuckoo clocks, popular from the 1870s. China ornaments were made in the thousands by pottery factories such as Minton and Doulton. Very popular were little statues or busts (head and shoulders only statues) of celebrities such as the Italian leader Garibaldi or the highwayman Dick Turpin.

The aspidistra

The aspidistra or '**cast-iron**' plant was a favourite Victorian house plant, often sprouting from a large china pot. Rather gloomy-looking, with long, dark leaves, it could survive almost any ill-treatment. It did not mind dingy corners, dust or smoky rooms, and stayed green all year round. You can still buy aspidistras today, although they are not so popular as they were with the Victorians.

This Victorian sitting room looks very crowded and full of ornaments, but it was the style at the time. Dusting must have been difficult!

Decoration

Thick curtains helped to keep out draughts in rooms heated by only a single coal fire. Most people thought staircarpets a luxury, as were fitted carpets. A large rug was better, since it could be moved around as it became worn. From the 1860s many people bought the new floor-covering called **linoleum.** It came in different patterns and was easily cleaned with a mop.

Victorian wallpaper was often patterned with pictures of flowers. Poor people stencilled pictures on plain plastered walls, because wallpaper was too expensive. In the 1850s, new machines began making cheap wallpaper. Just like today, people worried about being in or out of fashion. Charles Locke Eastlake, a writer with firm ideas about 'good taste', wrote in 1868 that he was pleased to see wallpaper becoming less flowery and that 'portraits of the Bengal tiger no longer appear on the domestic hearthrug'.

Heat and light

Every family liked a fireplace, and needed a fire to help keep out the cold. A few rich Victorian homes had central heating by the 1880s, but most people had open fires. The main fuel was coal, although Cassell's *Book of the Household* told readers that 'gas stoves … save an enormous amount of time and trouble, especially early in the morning'. The fire in every room had to be cleared of ashes, re-laid and lit every day.

Smoking away

Alice Foley remembered growing up in Lancashire in the 1890s. Her fireplace had a 'wooden shelf with a faded brocade pelmet [a decorated strip of cloth]. This served to hide a string stretched across the range from which hung damp stockings and handkerchiefs'.

People burned coal most of the year in stoves, kitchen **ranges** and fireplaces. Millions of chimneys puffed out vast clouds of smoke, ash and soot. Coal fires helped make the 'pea-soup' fogs for which London and other cities became famous.

The fireplace was the central feature of the room. When its fire was lit, people sat around it, looked into it, and warmed their backs by standing in front of it.

Keeping warm

Houses were cold in winter, so the Victorians wore more clothes indoors than we do today. Some country people put hot fire-ashes into a small clay pot, and warmed their feet on it. Into their beds, people put metal warming pans filled with hot fire-coals, or **earthenware** hot-water bottles known as 'pigs'. Rubber hot-water bottles appeared in the 1890s.

Gas lamps and oil lamps

By the 1840s, many houses had gas lamps, burning coal gas piped into homes from 'gas works'. In 1885, an Austrian named Carl Auer von Welsbach invented a new lamp with an 'incandescent mantle'. This glowed white hot, giving a soft, steady light. Later gas lamps lit automatically from a permanent 'pilot' light, when a small chain was pulled. Table lamps and carrying lanterns burned oil, drawn up into a cotton wick. At bedtime, many Victorians lit candles. They liked paraffin wax candles, which were less smelly than the old beeswax or tallow candles. After 1900, more homes had electric light, although many still used gas to cook and heat water.

This Victorian lamp stood on a table and would have been used for reading.

Switching to electric light

The first electric light bulbs were invented in the 1870s by Thomas Edison in the USA and also by Joseph Swan in Britain. Earlier experiments with electric light had produced blinding flashes, not much good for reading! For some years many Victorians stuck with gaslight, fearing electric light might damage their eyes. However, electric lighting began to be widely used in the 1880s.

The privy and the tub

As late as 1880, many Victorian homes were being built without bathrooms. Most people washed in the kitchen, at an outside water pump, or in basins resting on bedroom washstands. Few people had indoor toilets. Outside toilets, called 'privies', emptied into holes in the ground which were known as **cesspits**.

The Great Stink!

The privy was a deep hole with a wooden seat fixed across it. The hole was emptied every six months. It could get smelly even though most people did their best to keep the privy clean.

Indoor toilets were no good if there was nowhere for the waste to go. In 1858, so much filth flowed into the River Thames that Londoners called it the year of the 'Great Stink'. This meant that diseases such as typhoid were common – Prince Albert died from typhoid in 1861. Something had to be done. The engineer Sir Joseph Bazalgette built London's new **sewer** system, called 'the most wonderful work of modern times'. Completed in 1875, it had 134 kilometres of main drains and 1700 kilometres of local sewers. Much of the system is still in use today.

This picture of a Victorian water closet is from a catalogue published about 1890.

The triumph of the W.C.

Thomas Crapper and Frederick Humpherson were neighbours as well as business rivals who in the 1860s sold new water closets, or flushing toilets. Crapper showed his best model to Queen Victoria herself. Humpherson invented the 'U-bend' to stop bad smells seeping back up the pipe. His 'Beaufort Original Pedestal Washdown Closet' was sold in four styles: for 'Officers, Men, Servants and Convicts'!

Bath time

For washing, many poor people collected rainwater in barrels. In other homes with no piped water, people took water from an outside pump or well.

At bath time, about once a week, people sat in a small metal bath in front of a warm fire, behind a screen or a **towel horse**. The bath was filled with hot water carried from the kitchen. Big houses had more luxuries. In 1856, the comic writer R S Surtees described a bedroom with 'hip-baths and foot-baths, a shower-bath, and hot and cold baths adjoining and mirrors innumerable'. By the 1870s, piping water to a bathroom was cheaper than paying a servant to carry it. *The Builder* magazine of 1879 told readers that most homes had 'some dressing room or small room, where hot and cold baths can be placed' and that most 'respectable tenants' would pay extra **rent** of £5 or £10 a year for a bathroom.

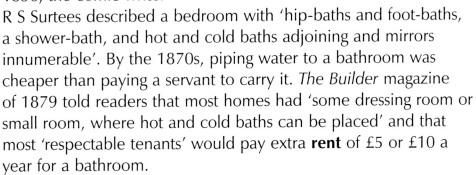

From the 1870s, Victorian plumbers were kept busy fitting baths and pipes into homes that had never before had running hot and cold water. This late Victorian bathtub was available from its makers with a shower.

People took cold baths more often than hot ones, until the invention in 1868 of the gas geyser. This was a gas-burning heater that gushed steaming hot water. Heavy **cast-iron** bathtubs, with taps and connected to proper drains, became popular from the 1880s.

The kitchen

The Victorian kitchen was ruled by women, either housewives or paid cooks. In poorer homes, the kitchen often doubled as the living room.

The kitchen range

Heat came from the coal-burning **range**, which was a big iron stove. Its fire heated an oven on one side, a water tank on the other, and a hotplate on top for pans and kettles. The range or 'kitchener' was the cook's pride and joy. The oven had no temperature control – those cooking just judged when food was ready. Some poor homes had no oven, so people took meat or pies to be cooked by the local baker. By 1900, the gas range and smaller gas cooker had arrived, saving the trouble of lighting a coal fire.

Gleaming pans and cookery books

Most kitchens had a food cupboard or a small room known as the pantry. On the wooden kitchen shelves, well-scrubbed iron and copper saucepans were ranged alongside frying pans, **skillets**, sieves, jelly-moulds, milk bowls and preserving jars for jam and bottled fruit. Meat and fish were eaten fresh, since until the 1870s there were no refrigerators to store food. Tinned meat, from Australia, first went on sale in British shops in the 1870s. In hot weather, people covered foods to keep the flies off it.

Kitchen gadgets

The Science Museum in London has a food processor from 1850, which shows that the Victorians were eager to try out kitchen **gadgets**. In the kitchen there might be apple corers, cherry pippers, knife polishers and tin openers.

Most cooks had their own family recipes, but also tried new dishes from cookery books. Eliza Acton had wanted to write poetry, but was told a cookery book would sell better. Her popular *Modern Cookery for Private Families* (1845) listed ingredients and explained how long each dish took to prepare. Food preparation took up a lot of time.

The range, with its oven and water heater, was the heart of the Victorian home. It also helped make the kitchen the warmest room in the house.

Many people made their own bread, biscuits and cakes, jam, bottled fruits and wine. Well-off housewives took pride in their stock cupboard, with its hams, nuts, herbs, apples and cheeses sitting on shelves.

Washing up and washday

Dirty dishes and pans were washed in bowls with bars of soap or soap flakes. Knives were rubbed clean with sand inside a sandbox. Some kitchens had a separate room called a **scullery**, with a big sink and a wooden tub or metal **copper** for the family clothes wash. Clothes were washed by hand, by pummelling them with a heavy wooden paddle, and scrubbing them against a ribbed wooden washboard. Rich people sent their washing to a laundry or employed a washerwoman. Washday was usually once a week, though some households did an enormous wash once a month.

Mealtimes

Mealtimes were important family gatherings. Victorian photographs and paintings show **middle-class** families gathered around the dining room table for meals. Dishes were placed on the **sideboard**. The father sat at the head of the table, carving the joint of meat on to plates, which were then passed around to each person.

Starting the day

Breakfast in better-off households was often a large meal, of rolls, bread, eggs, bacon, ham, cold meat and kedgeree – a dish of smoked fish and rice. There were no breakfast cereals until the end of the 19th century, though lots of people ate porridge. Before breakfast, one of the parents might say 'grace' or prayers. The servants, too, were expected to stand with head bowed or kneel, while prayers were said. A maid might serve the food, although for breakfast people often helped themselves from the dishes on the sideboard.

Poor people ate all their meals in the kitchen, or in the little parlour next door. Breakfast was eaten hurriedly before walking to work. It might be a slice of bread and **dripping**, with a mug of tea.

Lunch was usually a light snack. Working men took bread and cheese, or a meat pasty, to eat for their midday dinner. In middle-class homes, tea was served in the afternoon between 4 and 5 p.m., and the main meal was dinner in the evening. Children usually ate their supper in the nursery.

Charitable soup

Nearly every Victorian cookery book had a recipe for 'charitable soup'. Rich people made it with leftover meat and vegetables, and took the soup as a gift to poor families. The French chef Alexis Soyer, who cooked in a London gentlemen's club, took soup to Ireland to feed people who were starving during the potato famine of 1847–48.

Setting the table

A middle-class family's table would be covered with a thick undercloth, and a fine linen cloth on top. The cutlery would be of Sheffield steel or silver, with perhaps brass or even silver candlesticks, and glass decanters and jugs for wine and water. The plates and cups might be a full set of Staffordshire china. Poor families could not afford a fine linen tablecloth. They ate from tin or enamel plates, or cheap pottery. Cheap 'silver' cutlery became popular from the 1860s with the use of electroplating. This is a chemical process that adds a thin layer of silver to metal knives, forks and spoons.

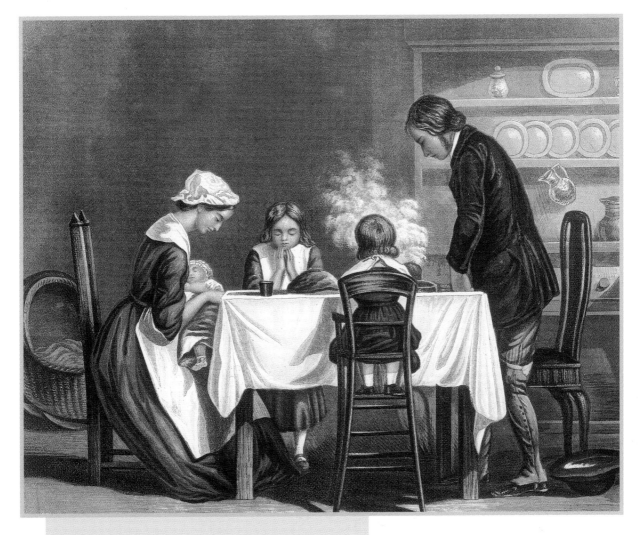

This picture shows a country family saying grace before a meal. Notice the child's high chair, the mother's cap and the father's gaiters (leggings).

Housework

Housework was women's work in Victorian times. Many women at home spent much of the day buying, preparing and cooking the family meals, as well as cleaning the house. Most of the work was done by hand. Some had servants, but many did it themselves.

A maid's work is never done

In the 1870s, a writer named Mrs Caddy listed the things a housemaid would need: black lead (for cleaning stoves and grates), starch, matches, hammers, pincers and nails, carpet tacks, feather brush, mattress-brush, wicks for lamps, twenty or so dusters, cleaning cloths, dust-sheets (to cover furniture), a window-rubber (for cleaning windows), 'lamp cloths' and sponges.

There was a lot of cleaning and dusting to be done in a Victorian home. This woman is cleaning the kitchen range.

The cookery book writer Mrs Beeton, writing in 1859, suggested a housemaid should start by 'opening the shutters and (weather permitting) the downstairs windows, clearing and lighting the kitchen **range** and dining room fire, dusting the dining room (not forgetting chairlegs), laying the table for breakfast, sweeping the hall and front doorstep, polishing the door-knocker, cleaning any boots – and then cooking breakfast'!

Battling the dust and creases

Poor women without servants brushed, scrubbed and dusted their often tiny rooms, using mops and brooms. Those who were 'houseproud' (and there were many) scrubbed the front step and polished windows with newspaper and vinegar. Mats and carpets were hung on a line to be beaten with what looked like a big fly-swatter that shook out the dust. Curtains and outdoor clothes too thick to wash were brushed and then sponged. Curtains might be cleaned once a year, as part of 'spring-cleaning'. This was a chance to open windows, air the house, and brush away the grime of winter.

Washday meant more hard work. Most people still did their washing by hand in a washtub. Men's collars and women's petticoats were treated with **starch** to stiffen them. Woollen and cotton clothes were creased after washing and so needed ironing. Heavy metal flat irons were heated by the fire. Box-irons were heated by putting a hot brick from the fire inside the 'box'.

Mousetraps and flypapers

The Victorian housewife set traps for mice and rats. She also waged war on flies, beetles, clothes moths and cobwebs! There was a saying that bedbugs 'bit all persons the same', and shops sold bed-bug traps. To catch flies, people hung up strips of sticky paper. The fly landed on the paper and got stuck. When there were lots of dead flies on the paper, you threw it away. Flypapers worked, but did not look very nice!

New gadgets for the home

In the constant battle against dirt and dust, Victorians found help in new **gadgets**. Machines were cheaper than servants. As the 19th century drew to its close, there were just not enough servants to go round, so more and more people bought 'household appliances'.

Sweeping and washing

The first mechanical carpet sweeper appeared in 1876. It was invented by an American, Melville Bissell, and had brushes that turned around as it was pushed along. It was another ten years before anyone had electricity at home, to power cleaners. The Bissell sweeper was followed by an air-blowing cleaner. This machine used a hand-worked **bellows** to blow dust out of dirty carpets and curtains. By 1901, electricity was being put into the homes of rich families. Some people showed off their new electric vacuum cleaners, which sucked up dust, rather than blowing it everywhere.

The first washing machines worked by turning a handle and went on sale in the 1850s. A non-electric dishwasher appeared in 1886. It was invented by a woman named Josephine Cochrane – to reduce the amount of crockery broken by clumsy servants! The electric iron appeared in 1882, and the electric washing machine in 1901. Like many household gadgets, all these were American inventions.

THE TORPEDO WASHER

CLOTHES CLEANED BY COMPRESSED AIR.

PATENTDE AND REGISTERED.   TRADE MARK—TORPEDO WASHER.

No Gas
No Steaming
No Dollying
No Steeping
No Preparation

No Tearing
No Entangling
No Bleaching
No Destruction
Great Saving of Soap.

PRICE LISTS AND TERMS ON APPLICATION.

Clothes Cleaned in one half the Time of any other Washer.
ADDRESS—

THE TORPEDO WASHER CO.
LORD STREET, HUDDERSFIELD.

This magazine advertisement was made to sell a new washing machine. People read about all kinds of new 'labour-saving' gadgets and were keen to try them.

Electric light had begun to replace gas by the end of the 19th century. At first many people found the new light bulbs much too dazzling!

A new world of gadgets

Advertising in magazines and newspapers helped to sell all kinds of new devices – from portable stoves for use outdoors to improved mousetraps and coffee grinders. Many people were wary of the new marvels. In *Little Women*, written by Louisa M Alcott (1868), Hannah (the servant) comes in with a letter for Mrs March: '"It's one of them horrid **telegraph** things, mum" she said, handling it as if she was afraid it would explode, and do some damage.'

From the 1890s people gradually got more used to electricity in the home. It brought the marvels of electric light, the telephone and plug-in electrical appliances.

Hanging on the telephone …

The telephone was invented in 1876. It was to change home life for ever because it meant families could speak to each other, but not everyone was impressed at first. The writer George Bernard Shaw was hired to tell people about the new invention, but he disliked it: 'It bellowed your most private communications all over the house instead of whispering them.' London's first telephone exchange was opened in 1879. By 1890, a person in London could call a friend in Birmingham.

Relaxing at home

Victorians wanted home to be peaceful and relaxing, a place where they could forget the cares of the world. In those days there was no television or radio, so people at home made their own amusements.

Reading together

Reading aloud was a popular **middle-class** family pastime. All the family would gather in the evenings to hear father, mother or an older child read from a novel such as Robert Louis Stevenson's *Treasure Island*. In religious households, the Bible would be read aloud and family prayers said each day; but there would be no work or games on Sunday.

Father was also first to read the daily newspaper, though he might share with others the bits he thought everyone should hear! Serious readers went to the lending libraries for books. Others chose the thrills of cheap novels and magazines, full of shocking scandals or bloodthirsty murders.

Games, concerts and quiet pleasures

Victorians were playful, enjoying all kinds of games, indoors and out. They liked card games, though gambling (playing for money) was frowned upon in respectable homes. Whist was a popular card game, while many children enjoyed the new favourite, Happy Families. Rich people with large gardens played summer games of tennis, badminton or croquet on the lawn. Poor children were chased outside to play football or cricket in the alley or street.

The scrapbook

Many Victorian children, and some adults, kept scrapbooks into which they pasted cut-out pictures of various things such as flowers, animals, famous people, or other things that took their fancy. Shops sold ready-cut pictures, which just had to be pressed out of a large sheet and stuck down. Some people put photographs or pressed flowers in their scrapbooks, too.

The Victorians made their own home entertainment – this family is playing a game called *Snapdragon*.

Home concerts and acting games, such as charades, were always popular. Sales of sheet music were huge. Many people loved to sing the popular songs of the day, often around a piano at home. There were no records until the last 20 years of the 19th century, so people sang, played and danced to their own music.

There were quiet hobbies, too, such as drawing and sewing. Many children learned to embroider by making samplers. A sampler was a piece of embroidery worked using various stitches to practise them. Victorian sketchbooks and embroidery can be seen in many museums today. Home dressmaking grew popular, as more people bought the new sewing machines, first sold by the American Isaac Singer in 1851. Paper patterns (showing how to copy fashionable styles) went on sale in 1863.

The Victorian garden

Victorians had firm ideas about gardens. They liked them neat, with trimmed hedges, gravel paths, flowerbeds and vegetables in rows. They also liked well-cut lawns. For the first time, houses in the **suburbs** had gardens at the front as well as at the back.

A trimmed lawn …

Until the invention of the lawnmower around 1830, most lawns were shaggy, not neatly trimmed. Grass was cut by men with long **scythes**, or by grazing sheep. A big machine at first, the lawnmower was soon made small enough to push. It produced a flat, shorn surface, ideal for garden games.

… and exotic plants

Victorian gardeners grew fruit and vegetables to eat, as well as flowers for the home. They were organic gardeners, using only natural fertilizers. They also set about breeding new varieties of common plants. Gardeners were keen to grow exotic plants brought back from all over the world. Victorians planted trees from North America, flowers from South Africa and shrubs from Asia. Some of their imported plants, such as the rhododendron, have gone wild and are now sometimes seen as a nuisance.

In their gardens, Victorians liked statues, stones, rockeries and sundials. After a government tax on glass ended in 1845, some people could afford large glasshouses in which to grow warmth-loving exotic plants such as cocoa palms, banana trees and tropical water lilies.

The Victorian gardener

Planting, said the Victorian gardener, was easy. The art was in training and pruning plants to shape, to make the garden look well turned out. This made some gardens appear rather too neat! From about 1890, garden designers, including Gertrude Jekyll (1843–1932), urged people to try a more wild and 'natural' look, with moss-covered steps, and summerhouses.

A nation of gardeners

Gardens ranged in scale from large areas of parkland, with lakes and small woods, to tiny cottage gardens – all flowery and overgrown, the kind that Victorian artists loved to paint. Even in grimy industrial towns, people grew plants in pots and window boxes. After all, many townspeople had come from the country or were the children of country people. They valued the greenery of city parks, too.

Gardens were also useful for growing food. Many houses had part of the garden set aside for fruit and vegetables. In 'the kitchen garden', people grew potatoes, onions, peas, carrots, cabbages and other vegetables, as well as herbs, strawberries, raspberries, apples, plums and pears.

This picture shows a family enjoying the warmth of a summer afternoon in their garden.

How do we know?

❖ ❖

There was a great difference between the neat and tidy **middle-class** Victorian home and the worst houses of the very poorest in the land. In 1848, a new organization set up to campaign for better housing heard that 'the air we breathe may be poisoned … The dwelling of every family ought to be provided with receptacles for all refuse and a good drain.' Better housing did come, and by 1900 telephones, hot water and warm radiators were becoming more commonplace in the home.

Victorian houses are still with us, in our cities, towns and villages. Some are grand houses; others are ordinary townhouses in **terraces** and squares, or small country cottages. Many are still family homes today.

We can wander through Victorian rooms, packed with objects, carefully recreated in museums and houses now open to the public. This is a small sitting room in Osborne House, Queen Victoria's house on the Isle of Wight.

Some Victorian furniture has also survived, much of it handed down through the generations. The finest pieces of Victorian furniture have become valuable **antiques**, but a surprising amount of everyday tables, chairs and **sideboards** can still be found in use.

Evidence in pictures and sound

The Victorian age was the first in history to leave us evidence in the form of photographs, moving film and crackly sound recordings. The early photographers of the 1840s took posed pictures of people at home. Cameras were taken into every room of the Victorian house, and into the garden, too. So we can see exactly what they looked like. There are also detailed paintings that show the colours of furnishings, rugs and clothes. We can still study illustrations from Victorian magazine advertisements and catalogues.

Written evidence

As well as photos, the Victorians left a huge mass of government reports on slum housing and 'improvement schemes'. Since 1801, a national **census** has been carried out every ten years, providing new information on how people lived. From records kept by the owners of houses and by building firms, we can see how houses were built, how much repairs cost and how much servants were paid.

Look around and learn

Can you find a Victorian house near you? The builder may have left his mark and a date on the outside. Most small Victorian houses have now been modernized, but many retain original features, such as windows and ceiling decorations. Even if you live in a modern home, you should now feel able to recognize lots of Victorian details in buildings and homes around you.

Timeline

1830 Liverpool and Manchester Railway opens. It is the first steam passenger railway
The lawnmower is invented

1837 Victoria becomes queen

1845 New wood-carving machines make **factory**-made furniture cheaper

1851 The **Great Exhibition** is held in London
Hand-turned washing machines go on sale

1858 Work gets under way to improve drains and **sewers** in towns

1859 First oil well sunk in the USA; petroleum oil is sold for oil lamps

1864 Water closets become more popular

1865 London's new sewers are opened
Octavia Hill sets up a housing scheme for the poor in London

1868 New laws under the Artisans' Dwellings Act allow local councils to demolish 'insanitary' homes (**slums**)

1870s Cuckoo clocks become popular in Britain

1875 Public Health Act sets minimum standards for homes, especially ventilation and drains
Local councils given powers to clear slum districts

1876 Alexander Graham Bell invents the telephone

1879 Edison and Swan each demonstrate an electric light bulb

1881 First electricity generating station in Britain opened at Godalming in Surrey
Portable oil heaters for warming bath water go on sale

1885 Karl Benz of Germany builds the first motor car

1887 Queen Victoria's Golden Jubilee (50 years on the throne)

1890 New 'garden suburb', with planned streets, trees, open space and middle-class housing, built at Bedford Park, in west London

1897 Queen Victoria's Diamond Jubilee (60 years on the throne)

1900 Gas-fired cooking **ranges** are hugely popular

1901 Queen Victoria dies. Her eldest son becomes King Edward VII

Sources

Sources

Dickens' London, Peter Ackroyd (Headline, 1987)

The English Country Cottage, R J Brown (Robert Hale, 1979)

Historic Houses of Britain, Mark Girouard (Artus, 1979)

Lark's Rise to Candleford, Flora Thompson (1945, first published as *Lark Rise* in 1939)

Oxford Illustrated History of Britain, Ed. Kenneth O Morgan (Oxford University Press, 1984)

A Social and Economic History of Industrial Britain, John Robottom (Longman, 1986)

Victorian Architecture, Roger Dixon and Stefan Muthesius (Thames and Hudson, 1985)

The Victorian House, John Marshall and Ian Wilcox (Sidgwick and Jackson, 1986)

Victorian Things, Asa Briggs (Penguin, 1990)

Victorian Village Life, Neil Philip (Albion Press, 1993)

Further reading

Victorian Britain, Andrew Langley (Heinemann, 1994)

Also, look on www.heinemannexplore.co.uk for more information on the Victorians.

Places to visit

Apsley House (Wellington Museum), London

Castle Museum, York (reconstructed street)

Cragside House, Morpeth, Northumberland

Ironbridge Gorge Museum, Ironbridge, Shropshire

London Museum, Victoria and Albert Museum, London

Museum of English Rural Life, Reading

New Lanark Visitor Centre, Lanark

North of England Open Air Museum, Beamish, Co. Durham

Osborne House, Isle of Wight

Shugborough Estate, Stafford (restored estate)

Waddesdon Manor, Buckinghamshire

Weald and Downland Museum, near Chichester, West Sussex

Welsh Folk Museum, St Fagans, Cardiff

Glossary

antiques old things that people today like to buy

bellows air pump for puffing air into something

billiard room room used to play the game of billiards

British Empire countries ruled by Britain or linked to it (from the late 17th century to the mid-20th century)

cast iron iron poured into moulds while hot and liquid, which hardens as it cools

census population count which collects information about people

cesspit hole used to collect toilet waste

cholera dangerous infectious disease carried by bacteria in polluted water

copper large wash-tub for boiling clothes, made of copper metal

conservatory greenhouse-like room for potted plants

dressing room small room for getting dressed and undressed in

dripping melted fat from roasted meat, allowed to cool and set

earthenware cheap kind of pottery

evidence picture, writing or a person's account, which tells us what things were like at a particular time

factory building for making goods, containing machines, materials and workers

farm labourer person who did heavy work on a farm

gadgets devices invented to make jobs easier or faster

gramophone machine invented in the late 1800s for playing records of music and speech

Great Exhibition festival of arts, science and industry held in Hyde Park, London, in 1851

gunroom room where shotguns and rifles used for hunting were kept

hoist small lift worked by hand or an electric motor

Industrial Revolution changes in manufacturing beginning in the 1700s with new machines for spinning and weaving, and the first steam-driven machines

linoleum hardwearing floor-covering made in a factory, using fabric, oil and resins

local council group of people elected to run a city, town or county

medieval means to do with the Middle Ages (roughly AD 500 to 1500)

middle class people in-between the rich and poor; in Victorian times, someone who ran a small business, for example

paraphernalia personal belongings or equipment; the word usually describes a lot of things packed together

parlour room where Victorians entertained their guests

patchwork quilt bedspread made from squares of material sewn together

pewter metal made from a mixture of lead and tin

privy outside toilet, usually in a small shed or outbuilding

range iron cooker heated by a coal fire

rent money paid by someone living in a house to the owner of the house

rush mat floor mat made from woven reeds

scullery small room with a sink, used for washing-up

scythe long-handled tool with a curved blade, used for cutting grass or wheat

sewer drain or system of pipes for carrying toilet waste away

sideboard piece of furniture for storing plates, cutlery and tablecloths, and also as a serving place for dishes during mealtimes

skillet small long-handled cooking pan

skirting strip of wood or other material laid where floor and wall join

slums poor areas of bad housing, lacking proper sanitation and clean water

starch means to stiffen; clothes (collars, for example) were soaked in starch, made from a substance found in rice and potatoes

suburbs residential areas a little way out from the centre of town

telegraph electrical instrument for sending messages along a wire

tenement tall building with stairs and small rooms, each with a family living in it

terraced house house attached to other houses in a row

thatch straw or reeds used to cover a roof

towel horse wooden folding frame for drying and airing towels

workhouse hostel for the poor and jobless, where residents had to work

Index